T0210072

My Life
Before
my Death
at
Seven Years Old

THOMAS GREEN

authorHOUSE®

AuthorHouse™
1663 Liberty Drive
Bloomington, IN 47403
www.authorhouse.com
Phone: 1 (800) 839-8640

© 2019 Thomas Green. All rights reserved.

No part of this book may be reproduced, stored in
a retrieval system, or transmitted by any means
without the written permission of the author.

Published by AuthorHouse 06/26/2019

ISBN: 978-1-7283-1692-5 (sc)
ISBN: 978-1-7283-1693-2 (e)

Print information available on the last page.

Any people depicted in stock imagery provided by Getty Images are
models,
and such images are being used for illustrative purposes only.
Certain stock imagery © Getty Images.

This book is printed on acid-free paper.

Because of the dynamic nature of the Internet, any web
addresses or links contained in this book may have changed
since publication and may no longer be valid. The views
expressed in this work are solely those of the author and do
not necessarily reflect the views of the publisher, and the
publisher hereby disclaims any responsibility for them.

INTRODUCTION

This story is about a seven year old boy. It is written by his father, who loved him all so much.

It tells the story of my life. My name is Tommy J. I could not write this story because of my death. It is a loving story, and I hope that everyone will buy, and read a very touching story. this book. Not only to yourselves, but read it to your kids. It is a story that everyone can, and will enjoy. I know it wasn't easy for my father to write this book, so please help to make it a success.

I left behind my father my mother (Felicia Green) my sister (Taormina Green, my brother (Joshua Green), and my brother (Bryant Green). I want all of you to know, I love you and I will always be in your hearts. Remember, I will see you again one day, in Heaven!!!

DEDICATION PAGE

I dedicate this book to my wife Felicia, and our kids Tori, Bryant, Joshua, and Skyy. I love you all dearly and my prayer is that you let God guide your steps, and watch what you can accomplish in life.

CHAPTER ONE

Hi! My name is Thomas Bernard Green Jr. I'm named after my father, who I am very proud of. All my friends call me Tommy J. My mother gave me that nick-name. I was born on August 26, 1983, in the town of Derby, Connecticut. I weighed eight pounds, eight ounces. I was a bouncing baby boy. My parents are Thomas and Felicia Green. They said they were so happy when I came along because my dad wanted to have a junior. I was named after him and I didn't mind it.

My mother and father told me about my first year in this world. They said I was one of a kind. They told me that when I was six months old, I had so much hair on my head that they had to braid it. I can imagine how funny I must have looked. My mother said I was a fast learning baby. She said I caught on to things very easily. My dad said that he wasn't going to spoil me, but he did. My mom told me he tried not to but he just couldn't help himself. My dad was so proud and happy because he got to hold me when I was born before my mother did. So how could he resist spoiling me. My dad said it was just like being a kid in a candy store. Once he got what he wanted, he didn't want to let go. When a kid gets his candy, he holds on to it as tight as he can. My dad said it was almost the same way with him. When I was born, and he saw he had a son, he held on to me for dear life. My sister was very jealous when I came along. My mom told me how when I was about three months old, my sister tried to stuff a big green olive down my throat. It wasn't funny at the: time, but later on, my parents laughed at it. If you must know, I didn't hold that against her (smile). My dad said that his brother, my Uncle Ephriam, had his own nickname for me. Are you ready for this? He called me Cricket. My mom didn't really like that name, but she couldn't stop him from calling me that. When I grew up, I didn't mind him calling me Cricket.

After a while, my mom won the battle of the nick-names and my Uncle Ephriam started calling me Tommy J. That name stayed with me all through school, even to the end. We were living on Liberty Street in Ansonia CT. when I took my first steps. My father said that we were in the kitchen at the time. I was standing up holding on to the kitchen chair, and I saw another chair nearby. My dad said all of a sudden, I just let go of the chair I was holding and waddled over to the other chair. He called it waddling, but those were my very first steps. From then on, it was fun and games for me, but hand tapping for my mom and dad.

They said when I learned how to walk, I started getting into everything. I took my first steps at nine months old. I also went to my sister's Head Start graduation. I didn't know what was going on because I was only nine months old just know my sister was very happy. I know that my mom and dad were happy because they were taking pictures of her. I really knew they were happy when we got home, because there was a big cake at home on the table. That made my day. My mom said I enjoyed it because that was my chance to make a big mess and didn't have to worry about getting tapped. So I made the best of it, I got ice-cream and cake everywhere. Boy, did I have fun! By this time my mom was starting to really spoil me too! My dad told her she had to take some of the blame for me being spoiled. I had gotten so bad that my mom couldn't do anything without holding me on her lap. She carried me around outside, she held me in church, and she even held me while she would cook dinner.

My grandfather, Ephriam Green Sr., and my Uncle Ephriam, use to tell my mom all the time to put me down. My mom would just laugh and hold me even tighter. So now, my mom was holding on to me just like my dad did when I was first born. When they told me how I was when I was less than a year old, I couldn't believe it. I would laugh with them. My sister would sit there and say, "null remember". I told her she should remember because she tried to make me eat that big green olive (the olive that was almost bigger than my mouth - smile). When I was about eleven months old, my mom said that she would lay down on the bed with me, take my bottle from me, and put it in her mouth. Of course, she was just playing with me. I later saw the pictures that my dad took of me and my mom playing on the bed.

I laughed when I saw the pictures. Seeing how my mom was playing with me then, let me know how much she really loved me. I could see the love in her eyes. I was glad my dad took those pictures. It made me love them even more. If you could only have seen my mom. It was funny because she still had her hair rollers in. She couldn't believe my dad took her picture while she was dressed like that. She wasn't really mad at him, but she did wish she had some clothes on. My mom now looks back at those pictures and she really treasures them. She wouldn't part with them for anything. I really love my mom. I had her wrapped right around my finger (smile).

CHAPTER TWO

When I turned one year old, guess what my mom and dad did to me! They took me off the bottle. What can be worse than someone taking your bottle away from you! Think about it, here I sucked on my bottle for 2 months, then all of a sudden, my mom took my bottle away. I waited and waited and waited for my mom to give it back to me, but she never did. Instead, she came toward me with a glass.(well it was really a cup). She expected me to drink from it. So me thinking that I had my mom wrapped around my finger, I pushed the cup away. She, being the loving mother that she is, wouldn't give up. She kept on giving me that stupid cup. But I still had a few tricks up my sleeve. I was determined to get my bottle back. I took the cup and threw it on the floor. My mom picked it up and gave it back to me. Mom wouldn't quit and neither would I. I still had one more trick left. When she tried to give me back the cup, I looked at her and started crying. The more my mom said I wasn't getting my bottle, the more I cried. When she tried to give me that cup again, I cried even louder. The funny thing about me doing all that crying was that I cried myself right to sleep (smile). I really don't know who won that battle. She didn't give me that cup, and I didn't get my bottle either. I guess you can call it a tie.

You will be glad to know that in the long run, she won. She won because I did learn how to drink from that cup. Not only that, my mom taught me how to drink from a glass. I then was able to get back at her for making me drink from a cup and glass. What I would do is, whenever mom would give me something to drink, when I was finished I would take my glass and throw it into the sink that was fun. I got my mom back by braking some glasses. I thought I had the upper hand but she fooled me again. She went back to the hand tapping. Believe me, that got my attention real fast, I remember those taps. Mom had won the round, she had me in check.

After getting my hands tapped, she would put me in the bassinet. We had a bassinet instead of a crib because that's what mom wanted. I would rock and rock until I'd fall asleep. Then, that gave me an idea. I started rocking harder and harder everyday until I made the bassinet fall. I thought that was it for that bassinet, but my dad just butted in and put the whole bassinet on the floor (smile). They weren't playing fair. That was cheating.

After a while, I out grew that bassinet and moved onto a bed. The hardest thing about a bed being that young was staying on top of it. My mom and dad said that I was a wild sleeper. I rolled off of the bed a few times. After hitting the floor a couple of times, my dad put some pillows around the bed so that if I rolled off, I would land on something soft. Gee dad, you should have thought of that earlier (smile). Pretty soon, I became good at sleeping on a bed, but I was still wild. Can you believe my mom and dad gave me my very first chicken leg when I was one year old? Do you know what? It was good (smile). My dad said I would eat that chicken leg as if it was going to run away. He said that after I would finish eating all the meat off, I would suck on the bone and try to chew the bone. That must have been funny. Of course, at the time I was also - teething. I tell you, when those teeth start coming in, watch out. It hurts and they itch. My mom went out and bought me something to put in my mouth. It was a teething ring. She would take the teething ring and put it in the freezer for a little while, so that it would be nice and cold. Then she would take it and rub it on my gums. Oh, that felt so good. It felt so good that I would start yelling sometimes just so she would give me that nice, cold teething ring. My dad told my mom to make sure she brought my teething ring to church with us. It worked in church for a little while. After the coldness went away, I started to cry. My dad said that my mom had to take me into the back of the church where our pastor's office was and just after about every Sunday. It was like everyone would wait to see how long it was going to take before my mom would bring me to the back. Everyone use to laugh about it after church. Some of them called me the water baby. Why? Because I cried so much. One of the good things back then was that I was the only baby boy in our church at the time. Everyone else had girls or had no kids at all. My dad said that's when all the ladies in the church started to spoil me too. My dad didn't like that too much but it was too hard for him to stop them. He was out numbered (smile). It was kind of fun for a while being the only baby boy in the whole church. Then the fun and games were over. A few more baby boys came along in the church. It seemed like all the ladies were having boys. Soon there were a lot of boys in our church. I didn't like that too much but there was nothing I could do. My mom told me she was an usher in our church until she had me. Then she had to sit down because I was a handful.

Also, at that time, my dad was singing on the choir. He was good too. Well, so he told me (smile). Most of the times when my mom tried to usher, she would stand over by where I was sitting so I wouldn't cry. Guess what? It didn't work. She ended up just sitting down with me every Sunday. My mom really loved ushering, but she didn't mind too much because she loved me. so much. After a while, my dad said he left the choir because of his job. They had rehearsal on Saturday and my dad worked on that day. My dad said that even when he was on the choir, he would always be on the floor helping out the ushers. So after he wasn't with the choir, he became an usher. My mom sat down and my dad stood up. That gave my mom enough time to teach me how to behave while in church. Soon I stopped crying and sat up straight. Then my mom decided she would start teaching me how to go to the potty. If it wasn't one thing it was another.

When we were home, it seemed like she was the meanest mom in the world. She made me sit on this small little toilet. It felt like every time I turned around, she was putting me on the petty. I mean, after I ate something. After I drank something. After I would wake up. I was on there all the time. What made it even worse was that my dad felt he had to join in. Whenever my mom wouldn't do it or she was too tired to do it, my dad seemed like he enjoyed doing it. I know I must have hated for him to do it because my mom said my dad would spank me every time I wet my clothes or messed in my clothes.

I probably thought my dad was the meanest dad in the whole world. Later in life, I realized that he did it for my own good. If not, I would have been like some kids, four and five years old and still wetting the bed. I was glad my mom and dad did train me to use that potty. Mom and dad were so glad when I was trained, they said I would fall asleep on the potty all the time. Dad would always have to wake me up and take me off. That must have really been funny to see.

CHAPTER THREE

After being potty trained before I was two years old, my mom said I got my first burn. It was from some hot tea. My mom said she was in the kitchen with a friend having some tea and here I come being nosey. I tried to look in the cup from the floor but I was too small. So I reached up on the table and grabbed the tea cup and some of the tea spilled on my arm.- It wasn't a lot, but it sure did scare me. I could just hear my dad now. He probably said something like, "Ah ha, that's what you get. That will teach you not to grab stuff off the table". He said it in a loving way but you know what, he was right. I didn't grab anything off our table or anyone else's. My dad always had a way of not really getting mad but he would make sure you knew and understood what he was talking about. Now that's what I call a very caring and loving dad. He would rather get hurt before he would let me get Ort. What can I say? That's my dad. He's one of a kind.

One day, my mom and dad were in the kitchen and my mom said we' were getting ready to go somewhere. I must have been in one of my moods, because I was being bad. My dad thought it was kind of funny. He didn't know I was that stubborn. He said I was holding on to the kitchen table leg and my mom was in the kitchen telling me to, "Come here".

I would look at her and just stand there. I wouldn't move. 10 After a little while, my mom started to get a little angry. She stood up from her chair, looked at me, and I looked at her. She called me again. I still wouldn't move. By this time, my dad told me he was trying to hold back his laugh. My mom was serious. She had a serious look on her face. So did I. This time she called me again, but with a stern voice. She meant business. Why did I do that? My dad said my mom walked over to me and hit me on my bottom. She said, "Come here." I must have been very determined to win this battle because my dad said I just held on to the kitchen table for dear life. The more my mom spanked me, the tighter I held on to the table. My mom could not believe I wouldn't let go. Finally, she had to pull me away from the table. I had finally won a battle with my mom (or so I thought). My mom told me that she said she was determined to brake me from my stubborn streak. We laughed.at that. Well, you probably already guessed that my mom broke me from that stubborn streak. She had no more problems from me like that ever again.

After I had turned two years old, my dad seemed to be more patient with me. Mom said, out of all the kids in the area where we Itmed, my dad was probably the only father that really took time out with his son. My dad said, that just about every time he took me out for a walk, he would run into these certain church women. They really didn't say anything to him, they just looked at us and smiled. My dad said he guessed that they couldn't believe that he was one of the very few fathers that took the time to be with his son. That made mom feel real good. Later on, my dad told me that deep down inside, he felt he was the proudest dad in the world. He said he enjoyed every minute he spent with me. What a dad! At this time in my life, my mom and dad weren't married. We were all just living together. My mom said after a while, she joined our church. Her and my dad weren't hitting it off too good then. So my dad said he ended up moving out. He didn't abandon me though. Dad said he moved in with a friend of his for a while. Then he got his own apartment. He came to see me, my mom, and my sister everyday. He even let us stay with him every other weekend. My dad said he loved it. My mom must have really been praying for my dad because he finally started coming to church with us. Mom said it felt good having dad in church, and that we looked like a real family. Dad said he started to really get into it. He started coming to church every Sunday. Before he knew it, he was joining the church. My dad said it was strange. He said, every time he went to church, it seemed like the preacher kept looking at him. He said he started not to come anymore, but something kept drawing him to the church.

Later on, my dad said he was missing something in his life. That something was God. My mom and dad said things were looking pretty good then for them. There was still hope. Everybody would look at us in church on Sunday as though we were already married. Things looked good. They were getting along, and I was potty trained. So they decided to show off a little in church. My mom said she would send me to the bathroom by myself. She said everyone would look at me while I walked across the floor to the bathroom. They wanted to know where I was going. They couldn't believe I was so young and already potty trained and going to the bathroom in church by myself. That made my mom and dad so proud. They couldn't stop smiling. I didn't even know I was showing off. There were kids in the church a little older than me and they weren't potty trained yet. So all you mothers, train your kids at an early age. Now a days, kids are growing up smarter than ever. So put them to the test. At two years old, I wasn't only potty trained, but my sister started teaching me how to count. After I learned how to do some counting, she started teaching me my colors. Not only that, I also learned how to put on my own clothes. It rick took me some time, but I caught on. My sister was only six years old at the time. She was teaching me these things. My sister is a very smart girl and I love her. My dad was so surprised when he found out how much I had learned at an early age. He didn't know I knew so many things because I would be in the room playing school with my sister. He thought I was just playing, but I was in there learning. Thanks to my sister Taormina.

One day while me and my dad were up on the north end of town, he said we were at the park and I got on someone's big wheel and rode it down a small hill and ended up on the basketball court. He said I was so scared, I didn't know whether to cry or laugh. He said it was funny but at the time it happened, all he could do was pick me up and hug me so that I wouldn't cry. My mom, being the mother that she was, wanted to know where my dad was at. She wanted to know the reason I was able to go down that hill. She also wanted to know if I was hurt. My dad told her no. He Said I was more scared than anything. Now that's a mom. My mom. I guess the biggest event in my life back then was when my mom and dad got married. They told me I wasn't in the wedding, but I was there. When I was older, I looked at the wedding pictures and they were beautiful. My mom looked so pretty and my dad looked like he came off the top of a wedding cake. My mom and dad showed me some pictures of myself. I looked just like a little peanut. I couldn't believe they made suits that small back then. I even saw my sister Taormina, she really looked nice. There were so many people in the wedding pictures. After the wedding, my mom said that everyone went to the community center to eat for the reception. By the looks of the pictures, it seemed like everyone had a good time. Especially my dad. I saw a. picture of my mom and dad. He was smashing some cake in her face. It sure looked like fun. If only I could have gotten my hands on some of that cake. I probably would, have smashed it in my face for fun (smile). My mom and dad got married nine days before my birthday and five days before my sister's birthday. They were married on August, same and my birthday was August 26th.

CHAPTER FOUR

When I was three years old, my dad said I was getting ready for Head Start. They said I was more than smart enough to go then, but I had to wait until I was four years old. My folks were a little disappointed because they wanted me to go, but they waited patiently. While we all waited, my dad laid I continued learning to count and match my colors. One of Head Starts main requirements was that your child be potty trained. When I heard that word again, I said to myself, "OH NO! Not again." Then I remembered I was already potty trained. I didn't have anything to worry about. As time went on, I began to pick out some of my own clothes to wear. My mom said it was amazing because I was able to match my clothes perfectly. My dad was so glad. He said he would send me into the bedroom to get my clothes just to see if I could match them. Do you know what? I did it. Over and over again. I got pretty good at it. I even saw some pictures of myself getting dressed. I looked at my dad and just smiled. He said, "That's you", and I smiled even more. My dad and our pastor, Pastor Moore, became very good friends. He said' she would treat him as if he were her very own son. One day, my dad said he had to go over her house and so some painting. He said I was always up under him, so he had to take me with him. He said that when we got there, Pastor Moore wanted him to go a few places for her before starting to paint. He really didn't want to drag me all over town with him, in and out of stores. So my dad said that Pastor Moore said she would watch me. He said CK. She didn't know what she was getting herself into. Pastor Moore told my dad when he came back that I had talked her ears off. My dad told me I went all through her house asking her what everything was. He also told me that she took the time to explain everything to me. Even though she was tired, she talked to me. Me, a little three year old. My dad told me I really tired her out. She was so tired, she laid up on her bed, and made me lay up there too. He said he laughed. He thought that was funny. When I got older, I laughed at that too. My mom told me also, that when we were in church, Pastor Moore was on her way out and I yelled out, "Where you going Pastor Moore?" I think my mom was just as surprised as Pastor Moore. They both laughed.

There was another time when Pastor Moore gave me something for my birthday. I knew she was a nice lady but my mom said that I asked Pastor Moore where was Taormina's. When she told me that she didn't have one for her, my mom said I told her, "don't do that no more". They were both speechless. When my dad told me I said that, I couldn't believe it. Thank God my Pastor knew I didn't really know what I was saying. (smile)

My mom and dad use to take me and my sister to the park all the time. We lived right in walking distance. My dad said he loved to take pictures so much, that we all took pictures at the park. I also saw those. My mom didn't really like taking pictures but she had no other choice when she was with my dad. If she didn't want to take a picture, he would sneak one. The summer was going by quickly. My mom and dad said they wanted to take us somewhere before school started. I would be starting school this year. Guess where we went? We went to South Carolina to see my grandmother. I was too young to know who she was but my mom did tell me that it was her mother. My dad said that his mother had died when he was five years old. We went down there in August. If you remember, that's the same month as my mom and dad's wedding anniversary, my sister's birthday, and my birthday. You guessed it right. We spent all three of those special days down south. My dad said that we all had a wonderful time down there. He said we drove all the way. My mom said she hadn't seen her mother in a long time. She said that when we drove up the driveway, she was so happy to see her. My grandmother had seen me for the very first time. Taormina had seen her before but this was something new for me. I was afraid to go to her because I didn't know who she was. I really stayed away from her when I saw her dog. It wasn't a big dog but he was fast, he had teeth, and he liked to NMI on people. My mom said he was just a playful dog. I didn't care if he was playful or not. I was going to make sure he didn't jump on me. I made sure he didn't jump on me because wherever my mom went, I was right with her. I wasn't holding onto her leg because I knew the dog could get me. So where ever my mom went, she had to carry me. I didn't get enough courage my dad said until our vacation was almost over. We were down there for two long weeks. Those were the two longest weeks in my life. My dad said I didn't really start walking around the house until about four days before we came home. My mom said that overall, my sister and I had a good time. My dad said he took a whole lot of pictures but he left them down there by mistake. We never did get them back. My mom and dad said I was so glad to be back home where there wasn't any dogs, and I could run around the house without being chased.

CHAPTER FIVE

When we returned home from our vacation, it was time for school to start. Taormina wasn't ready to go back but, I was really happy. I had studied hard all summer and I was going to finally start school. "School", that sounded so good. My dad said Head Start will never be the same. My mom was just as happy as I was (maybe even happier). My mom said she dressed me nicely and we all waited impatiently. This was going to be my first time riding on a bus all by myself. Not just any bus, but a school bus. My dad said that if I could have seen the 'look on my face when I saw the bus. It wasn't just a school bus, it was a big yellow bus. Dad said, I put a smile on my face nice enough to light up the town. I saw a picture that my dad took of me that day. I was just about to step on the bus when he called me. As I turned and looked at him, he took my picture. I was still smiling. I must have worn a smile on my face all day. I also had my very own lunchbox (smile). As I got on the bus and took a seat, I made sure I sat right next to a window. I wanted to make sure I could see my dad out the window, when I looked, I smiled because he was standing right there. By this time, he was smiling just as much as me. When the bus started to drive away, I started waving to my dad. He smiled some more and was waving back to me. I was glad I was going to school, but I really didn't know what was waiting for me there. When I got there I didn't know what to do so I just went into the school with the rest of the kids. After I saw all the other kids there, I didn't feel so bad. I had a lot of fun that day. I met so many new friends, I couldn't wait to get home to tell my mom and dad. My mom said, as I was trying to tell them about my day in school, I was talking so fast, they couldn't understand everything I was-saying. They said I was so happy, I just couldn't tell them fast enough. My sister seemed happy too. Everyone was happy for me.

After having so much fun in school, I couldn't wait to go back the next day. My dad said he never saw a kid so happy to go to school. Most kids at that age still don't want to leave mama. When mom leaves them in the classroom, they start to cry like mad. I was glad to say that I didn't cry, not once. I guess I didn't cry because I was having too much fun. There were toys everywhere. I didn't know what to play with. They even had swings and bikes outside for later. Although I was having so much fun, I did have to learn some school stuff. I should have known that because my dad told me. I guess I got a little excited when I saw all those toys. But then what did you expect, I was only a kid. Kids are supposed to look for toys. That's the first thing we look for wherever we go (smile).

I had two teachers in my classroom. They were very nice. They didn't yell at us at all. We all learned a lot from them, and they were fun. When I would come home from school, my dad would be right there waiting for me to get off the bus. He would hug me and give me a kiss on the cheer. He would them ask me how my day was in school, and did I have fun. He would then ask me what I learned in school. After I told him, I would then give him a picture. I would make my dad something in school everyday, and give it to him when I got home. After a while, my mom started asking me where her picture was. So I started making something for her. My mom said she was glad to see me giving my dad something everyday. She said it felt good to see how much I loved my dad, and I did. My mom know I loved her just as much. After school, my dad wanted me to feel like a big boy so, he would send me to the store all by myself. We lived only four doors down from the store. What he would do was, he would stick his head out of our window and watch me as I went to the store. He never took his eyes off me except while I was in the store. When I bane out of the store, I would look up at our window and guess what? He would still be out the window waiting for me to come out. He did that with me just about everyday. I thought it was fun. It made me feel like a big boy.

When I got upstairs, I would always ask my dad how I did. He would always. smile at me and say, "You did a good job. You are a big boy now. Do you know what? I really felt like one. I loved doing things with myckd. School was really nice. It was so nice, we even ate lunch in there. One day our teacher asked us what we like to eat. After I told my teacher what I liked to eat, I added a little more. I told the teacher that my dad liked to eat cat food. The teacher looked at me and said, "Cat food?" I told her yes. It comes in a little can, and it looks like little hotdogs. I was lucky. I had a cousin that was a teacher there and she overheard what I had said. I looked at her and she was laughing. She told me and the teacher that it wasn't cat food, but that it was little sausages in a can. They thought it was so funny. I really thought it was cat food. The teacher that was my cousin told my dad what I said and he laughed. When he started laughing, I know for sure I wasn't it trouble. My mom laughed when she heard about it also. As time passed, and we were moving along in

Head Start, we were to bring one of our parents to school with us because we had fixed lunch for them. Everybody in my class brought their mom with them. I was the only one that brought my dad. My teacher said that we had a treat today because our parents were with us. Then she said we have a real special treat today because my dad was the only father that came. That made him feel good. It made me feel good too. Then, when it was time to eat, my cousin came over to the table and asked my dad, "Are you sure you don't want some eat food? They laughed. It was a joke that she never let him forget. As a matter of fact, from then on, whenever she saw him, she would look at him and say "meow". They would laugh by the time my graduation rolled around, my mom and dad had become foster parents for a little boy. His name was Bryant. I didn't know at the time that he was going to stay. I thought he was going back home. I didn't want him to stay because I wanted to be the only boy in the family. I got mad at him because he wouldn't leave. My mom told me I had to get used to seeing him because he wasn't going anywhere. I didn't know what it was but, I was jealous of Bryant. My mom said, whenever she would hold Bryant, I would get up under her and start acting like a baby. The way my mom got me use to him was, she would let me hold him at home. Not only at home, she-would let me hold him in church. After a while, I started to like him. When he got older and bigger, I started playing with him. We became buddies. As the school year was ending, we were preparing for our graduation. We were aiming to have it at a park. We were going to hate a picnic. When the day came for us to graduate, I was even happier... I was happy because my dad said I was going to a bigger school. Then I really knew I was turning into a big boy. My mom, dad, and my sister came to my graduation. Even Bryant came. Of course, you know my dad was taking pictures. When he got the pictures back, he showed them to me. They really turned out nice. There were some of me with my diploma, with my cap on my head, and with me eating a hotdog. I had a good time at the picnic. My mom and dad said, that was my day. I really enjoyed it. I didn't want it to end, but it had too. Head Start wasn't that bad after all (smile).

CHAPTER SIX

Wouldn't you know it, my mom said about two months after we had Bryant, she found out that she was going to have a baby. I was five at the time. She said she couldn't believe it. We did want to have another baby she said, but not that soon. My dad said he didn't know what to say or do. He said that after he cleared his head, he know they weren't going to get rid of it. Mom and dad said all they could do was prepare themselves for it. They had already fallen in love with Bryant and they weren't going to give him up. My brother Joshua was born in July, and it was hot. I wasn't at the hospital with my dad when he was born but, I did get to see him the next day. He looked so small. Now I knew this baby wasn't going to go anywhere. I knew he was coming home with my mom. My dad had already told me. After Joshy was born, I called him Joshy for short. Anyways, after he was born, I had to go and stay at a friend's house for a couple of days. My sister stayed at another house. We had to stay somewhere else at the time because my dad had to work. We were too young to stay at home by ourselves. We were gone for three days. Those were three long days. My dad did call us everyday. He called to see how we were doing, and then he would tell us that mommy and Joshy were doing fine. I knew they were coming home, but, it wasn't soon enough. I couldn't wait to get home. When my dad called me and said that mommy was coming home, he said I was so happy. I knew Taormina was happy too. I hadn't seen my sister for three days. We were glad to see each other. We hugged and smiled at each other.

When I finally saw my mom, I ran over to her, jumped in her arms, and squeezed her. I was more than happy to see her. Ta o r m i n a did the same thing. My mom said she was happy to see us, and that she missed us so much. We were just glad that she was home. She asked us how we were doing. Taormina said she was fine. My mom asked me how I was doing. She called me To m m y J. I told her I didn't ever want to go back to that house I stayed at again. When she asked me why, I told her. I told her that the two other boys that were there, were mean to me. My mom said, "What did they do to you?" I told her that when we were playing, they took me and put me in a closet and shut the door. It was dark in there and they wouldn't let me out. My mom asked me what did I do and' how did I get out. I told her I started crying, and when they heard me crying, they opened the door. After they opened the door, they started laughing at me. That hurt my feelings. My dad was mad. Not at me, but at them. My mom told me not to worry because she wasn't going to send me over there ever again. That made me feel much better. Then my mom told my dad not to say anything to the boy's mother. He was going to because that really made him mad. I was glad mom was home. Little did I know, that was the beginning of a new phase for me. I had almost forgotten about Joshy. Soon, every time I turned around, if my mom wasn't holding him, my dad was. After a while, I started feeling left out. It seemed like my dad, the one who use to do everything with me, had forgot about me now. I started getting mad. My mom told me, I was a very jealous son. She said, every time I saw her pick Joshy up, I would roll my eyes and turn my head. I didn't hate Joshy, it's just that he was now getting more attention than me. I was the only boy in the house until Bryant. It took me awhile to get use to him, but I did. Now here comes Joshy. Now there's three boys in the house. My dad did make me feel a lot better. He told me to remember, I was the oldest boy and that they were my little brothers. Soon they will be coming to me, their big brother for help. When he told me that, it made me feel pretty good. I would be able to teach them everything I already knew. One of my mom's ways of helping me get over my jealousy was by letting me hold Joshy on myilap. I remember her doing the same thing to me with Bryant. It worked with Bryant, and you know what, it worked again with Joshy. Before I knew it, I was buddied with Joshy too. He was just as much fun as Bryant.

My dad was always in a good mood. He was so happy things were going good. Me and Taormina took pictures with Joshy and Bryant. My dad was more than happy to take them. I had already started kindergarten, and was getting ready to go into first grade. My dad said, as I get into the higher grades, that the work would get harder. Fe also told me not to worry because I was a smart boy. My mom always thought I was smart too. After graduating from kindergarten, I began first grade. I had fun there too. I met some new kids, and some of the kids that were in my kindergarten class, wherein my first grade class. My teacher was very nice. The work wasn't hard at all. I really enjoyed doing the work. When I got my first report card, I got excellent marks. I even got some money for doing a good job in school. My sister got some money too. It was fun, we took pictures and everything. My mom and dad loved our class pictures.

Every morning, either me, or my sister, would help my mom walk' Joshy and Bryant down to the baby sitter. I think I went with my mom more than Taormina. I didn't mind. Taormina use to hate getting out of the bed. I walked back and forth from the baby sitter so much, it felt like I was wearing out my sneakers. I kept on asking my dad to buy me some British Knights, those are sneakers. They cost over sixty dollars. My dad saw how bad I really wanted them. So he told me, "Let's go for a ride". When we got to where we were going, he said, "Come on". I said, "Where are we going?" He said, "Didn't you say you wanted some British Knights?" I looked at him, smiled, and said yes. He then said, "Well let's go and get you a pair." When he had said that, I jumped up and said, "Alright". That made my day. I was so happy, I wanted to wear them home.

When I got home, I ran into the house and showed everybody my new sneakers. My dad said I was so happy, all I did was run around the house and outside all day. I kept that smile on my face. My dad said if I were able to sleep in them that night, I would have. He wouldn't let me though. I took good care of my sneakers. If anyone stepped on them, I would tell them to watch out. Then I would wipe them off. I knew that was over doing it, but they were mine. By now, I was already six years old and growing fast. I knew those sneakers weren't going to last. I was just a happy little camper. As time went on, school got even better. I started getting even better grades. I had to because, the better grades me and my sister got, the more money we got. We got five dollars for every "A", and one dollar for every "B" we got. Believe me, we made out pretty good. We tried to get all my dad's money.

CHAPTER SEVEN

After I had turned seven years old, my dad and I did even more things together. It was back to the way it was before Joshy and Bryant came along. I loved every minute of it. One day after my dad came home from work, he took me for a ride. He was managing a house in Oxford for the Mentally Retarded. I didn't know where we were going but, he took me to see the house. He loved his job. When we got there, I couldn't believe how nice it was. It was very big. He took me inside and showed me the whole house. He then took me out on the back porch. There was so much green grass all around the house. It made me want to play there all day. We didn't stay too long because his clients were going to be back home in a while. I did have a nice time seeing the house. I think it was a couple of weeks later when my dad took us all up to see the house. This time only my mom went in the house because his clients were home. My mom said she really liked the house. She said it was beautiful. She got to meet my dad's clients and everything. My mom saw one of them outside on the back porch, and she thought he was so cute. He would stand there and smile while he was rocking back and forth. She thought it was cute. My mom then got to meet the people that were working for my dad. Not all of them, but some of them. My dad use to kid around with her and tell her that he has all women working for him. So I guess it was only natural for her to want to see them, and she did. I don't think she worried about those women after that. My mom would tease my dad by saying, "Yes, I called your job and when one of your female staff answered the phone, I told them to tell you it's your wife. Just to remind them that you are already taken." My dad would laugh. My mom didn't like my dad working so hard. He loved his job but, my mom didn't want him to over work himself. My mom really loved my dad.

My mom had a thing of making up names for us. She gave all of us a nickname. My name was, Mr. Tiucklebee. Isn't that funny? I don't know where she got that name from, but whenever we were playing around, she would call me Mr. Hucklebee. I don't remember everybody's nickname, but I do know they were funny. I thought my mom was so nice, because she would take time out and read us a story. Or she would sit down and watch a TV show with us. Just by her doing that, I know how much she really loved us. She would even play board games with us. He said I was a poor sport because I would get mad when I was losing. Even though I would get mad when I was losing, deep down inside, I was having a lot of fun.

My dad was working so hard, it made it even more fun when he would sit down and play with us. It also made mom feel good to see dad playing with us. Bryant and Joshy were too small to play but, they were sitting right there while we were playing. They were having just as much fun as we were, in their own way. Little kids will make something fun. My mom and I were getting even closer. She had started teaching Sunday school. Whenever she would do her lesson at home, she would let me help her. That really made me feel good. After she'd finish, she would ask me if I liked it. She always said I was very blunt and honest. If I liked it then ok. If I didn't like it, I would just come out and say so. My mom was a very good teacher. I know it sounds like I'm bragging about my mom, but she is my mom. Not only that, but by now you should have guessed that I was in her class. I wasn't there just because she was my mom. I was in her class because she happened to be teaching kids in my age group. I thought it was pretty neat. I not only helped my mom, I also got to see the lesson before everyone else. It wasn't cheating, it's just that Moved Sunday school. Most kids sometimes think it's a place to fool around. I went to Sunday school to learn, and I did. I loved church just as much. Sometimes I would go home and play church with my sister and brothers. They loved church too. My sister and I were on the little kids' choir. We would sing one Sunday out of the month. After singing on the kids' choir for a while, I finally got to sing a lead song, "Let the Hallealuha's Roll Way Down in our Sanctified Soul". I really had fun singing that. My mom and dad were so happy for me when I came home from rehearsal and told them I was singing the lead song in church on Sunday. My dad said, "Alright". My mom said, "Go ahead Tommy J.". I was so happy, I kept singing that song in the house all week long. When the time came for me to sing, I stood there and sung my heart out. When it was over, everyone in church told me I did a good job singing that song. I went over to my mom and dad and they told me how proud they were. It felt good singing, and I couldn't wait to sing another song.

One Saturday night, my dad and one of our ministers, took me and some more boys from our church, to a pro-wrestling match. There was about nine or ten of us all together. It was my very first time going to a match. I always watched it on TV. To be there in person, made it even more exciting. I really had a good time. Even though I was one of the youngest there, I still had a lot of fun. My dad was great. He let me hang out with the older boys and he didn't yell at me, not once. He bought me whatever I wanted to eat. It didn't matter how much it cost. What really made my night was after the matches were over. Everybody was buying things to take home with them. I didn't have any money. So I asked my dad if he would buy me something. He said, "You think I would bring you to a wrestling match and not buy you something?" When he said that, I started smiling. We went over to the counter and my dad told me to get whatever I wanted I looked and picked out something with Hulk Hogan on it. My dad then looked at me and said, "Go ahead and get something else." You know what, I did. I got a stack of cups with wrestling men on each one. We then got back on the van and went home. When we got home, I showed my mom, my sister, and my brothers what I had bought at wrestling. They smiled and said, "Wow. That's nice." My dad had made my night. I couldn't wait to go again. All the other kids had a ball while we were there. They laughed and jumped up and down. They had a great time. They wanted to know when we were going to go again. We didn't go for a while. So I just hung out with my dad. We would drive around here and there. We would do this and that.

To some people, it may not seem like much but it meant a lot to me. I think it meant even more to my mom. She loved seeing me and my dad doing things together. I always wanted to go everywhere with him. Even if it was just to the store. One of the nicest things we did together as a family was; when we all got dressed up and took family pictures. My dad had just gotten home film work. My mom told him to hurry up, wash up, and get dressed, He said, "for what".

Mom told him we had to hurry up and get to that hotel that was taking family pictures. She said, "Remember". My dad said he forgot all about it. So he hurried up and we went to the hotel. When we got there, there were a few people ahead of us, so we waited. When our turn came, we all smiled and went in. The man taking the pictures was very nice. He said we were a very nice looking family. Mommy and daddy took some by themselves. They looked like they were having fun. Then I, Taormina, Bryant, and Joshy took some. We had just a little problem. Joshy started to cry and Bryant didn't want to smile. I took a little while before Joshy stopped crying. If you see the pictures, you'll see that Bryant still didn't smile. He just kept a serious look on his face. He looked like he meant business. After that, we all got together and took a family group picture. Joshy didn't cry anymore because he was sitting on daddy's lap. I guess he felt safe. Bryant at on daddy's other lap but he still had on his serious look. We even managed to get a smile out of Joshy. Taormina was having a good time, and so was I. She smiled, and smiled, and smiled. She really looked nice that day. We all did. I smiled, but I didn't show my teeth.' because I was missing some. Right in the front. I didn't want to mess up the pictures. It took a while for the pictures to come back, but when they did, they really looked nice. My mom and dad were very pleased with the outcome. They couldn't wait to hang them up. They put them up in our living room. The one thing about those pictures was that the background matched our new living room set. We got the picture back after we bought the furniture. Just our luck, it matched perfectly. Overall, I think we all had a pretty good time. My dad wasn't tired anymore. My mom was still in a good mood. Bryant and Joshy even seemed a little happier. Taormina, you couldn't tell her anything. She just knew she was looking good. Just kidding (smile). As for me, I can truly say, I really enjoyed myself. I always did enjoy taking pictures. I guess I'm just like my dad. I know he loves taking pictures, and having his picture taken. As time went on, my dad told me that another wrestling match was coming our way. I asked him if we could go. Fe said if he was able to get some tickets, he would take me. Fe then said that if we went, it was only going to be us two. It was going to be father and son night for us. I didn't mind. I loved hanging out with my dad. Time was still moving on when my dad came home and told me, "Come on". I asked him where we were going. He said we were going to get out tickets. I said, "To wrestling"? My dad said, "Yes", I started smiling and ran to get my jacket. We went to the box office to see if they still had tickets. As my dad stood at the window, and the man said "yes", I said, "alright". So my dad went ahead and bought two tickets. I was so happy. I thanked my dad. He said, "For what". I told him for buying the tickets. He looked at me and said, "Nothing's too good for my son". That really made me feel close to him. My dad and I were always close, but when he said that, it really did something to me. It was enough to make someone cry the way he looked at me, I knew he meant it. He really meant it.

Oh, how I loved my dad. I mean I really loved him.

The night for wrestling finally came. I was talking about it all day. I couldn't wait for it to get dark. Just before we left, my dad had to stop by the house. I went into the house with him. When we came back out to get in the car, we noticed that one of our windows was broken. It happened just that quickly.

We went in the house to use the bathroom. When we came out, that's what we found. The person that did it was just leaving.

My dad questioned him about it and he said he would pay for the window.

My dad went to a car wash and vacuumed all the glass out.

He then went to the store and bought some cardboard. He put it inside a plastic bag, and put it up .to the window. It didn't look great but my dad said it was good enough for now. He still wanted to take me to the match. We still made it over there in time. They were just starting when we took our seats. It felt good being there. Just me and my dad. After we saw a few matches, I leaned back, looked at my dad and said, "Dad I needed this", and smiled. He looked at me and said, "what, again". I said, "I needed this". My dad looked at me, rubbed my head and said to me, "you're a trip". He then started laughing. Little did I know, that was going to be our last time spending time together as father and son. I didn't realize at that time, I was saying good-bye to my dad. Me being young, I didn't know what was going to happen. Me being so young, how could I know?

Deep down inside, I believe my dad really knew how much that match meant to me. He not only heard it in my voice, he also saw it in my face. I believe that was the closest moment we ever .shared,, I'm not saying my dad and I never shared any close moments because we have. I am saying, the night of the match that was our final bonding. I know it sounds strange, but that was a bonding that will last forever. Even a few days later, I was still doing things with my dad, but that was the night.

My dad told my mom what I had said that night. She laughed.

She really didn't pay it any mind. She didn't have any reason to take it so serious. Later on, she understood why I said that and she then understood why my dad and I were spending so much time together. She didn't know what was going to happen.

I had caught a little cold, and I had stayed home from school for two days. I didn't mind because that gave me the chance to play with Bryant and Joshy. I was sick, but I was having fur while I was staying home.

After being home for two days, my dad said I was going back to school the next day. I looked at him and said, "Do I have to". He said, "Yes, you're not sick anymore". He then said, "I thought you like school". I told him I did. He asked why I wanted to stay home. I really didn't have a reason so I told him I wanted to play with Joshy and Bryant. My dad said, "You play with them everyday". Again he didn't know what was going to happen. I just wanted to spend some special time with my brothers.

My dad understood later, why I didn't want to go back to school right away. He then knew that was my way of saying good-bye to them. Still, I didn't know or understand what was going on. I thought I was just being me. I knew I loved my brothers and I always had fun with them. No one could take that away from me.

Taormina and I were always close. We fought just about everyday. We didn't fist fight, but we hit and pushed each other around a lot. We didn't try to hurt one another. That was just our way of showing our love. There's an old saying that, "the person you're always fighting, is the person you really love".

I can honestly say that is a true statement because I really did love my sister. I know that she really did love me. Our love for each other will never part.

One of the strangest things happened to me a few days before my untimely departure. There were other in the same building as us. For some reason, I waving to them and saying good-bye to them. At kids that lived found myself the time, they weren't going anywhere. I just didn't know what was going on, or what was going to happen. So I ended up saying good-bye, even to my upstairs neighbor. I know to some people it may seem a little scary, but only God knows what lies ahead. Maybe God had me saying all my good-byes then because he knew I would never see them again.

I had the most heartwarming and tear shedding moment in the world. Although I didn't cry at the time, if anyone reading this book had seen the moment I am about to explain, it would gaiatietkek02. Brought tears to your eyes. It is something I believe many parents have gone through, but at the time, they didn't understand what was going on.

The night before my accident, I had the chance to say goodbye to my mom. I didn't know I was saying good-bye and neither did she. My mom thought I was just being very affectionate, was always close to my mom, but this night was different from any other night. God had a way that is so sweet.

On this night, God had it so that both of my brothers had gone to bed early. Not only that, God had my sister go to bed early also. She was the type of person that always wanted to stay up late. They all were in bed early. My dad was sitting in the chair in the den watching TV. My mom was sitting on the couch in the den watching TV. I was sitting on the floor next to my dad watching TV.

I then got up, I went over to my mom and wrapped my arms around her neck. I just held her around her neck and wouldn't let go. She didn't know why I was doing that. She thought it was just because I loved her. I really did love my mom. She was the best mother a boy could ever have. That night, that wasn't the only reason I was hugging her like that.

God wanted me to share a very special moment with her. One that she would remember always.

As I was hugging her, my dad looked at us and said, "Look at you, you got mommy all to yourself". Not knowing why! He then said, "how about I go wake your brothers up so they could hold mommy too". Although I knew he was just kidding, I looked at him and said, "No". My dad then smiled and said, "Go ahead, you can have mommy all to yourself". Still only God knew what waited ahead for us. It was all in God's hands.

I continued hugging my mom. I then turned her face toward me and said, "Look at me ma". She looked in my eyes. I said, "I love you". That was my good-bye to my mom. Neither of us knew it at the time, but my mom understood that moment later.

If my mom had known what was going to happen, even if there was no way to stop it, she would have held me all night long.

I know that if my parents knew my time was up, they would have had me sleep with them. I would have love every second of it.

My parents were the best. They couldn't have done a better job raising me.

The night before our special moment, I was in the living room helping my mom with her Sunday school lesson. I turned and said to her, "Ma I want to be saved. I want to live right."

She didn't really think it was strange coming from me because she knew how much I loved God. My mom talked about God all the time. I guess I kind of surprised her when I said it but she didn't think it was strange. Later on, my mom pieced that together also.

The night of the hugging was not the last time I saN4my

family. My mom woke my sister and I up for school the next day.

It was as though everything was back to normal. We washed up and got drove for school. We ate breakfast and gave our mom and dad a kiss before we left. I didn't know that when I left the house that morning, that would be the last time I would see my mom, I never got to see her again. My sister walked me to school everyday because she was older than me. After she walked me to my school, she said, "See you later". I met her after school and we walked home together. She had to go to the library when she got home to do her homework. My dad wouldn't let me go with her that day. Not knowing God wanted me to stay home.

Ta o r m i n a was at the library and my mom was at work. Joshy and Bryant were playing in the house. My dad was in his bedroom. I asked my dad if I could go outside and he told me to wait for my mom to come home. My mom was late coming home. She had called my dad and told him that she would be home in a little while. She had went to the store to get something for dinner.

I was getting tired of waiting. I was mad at my dad because he told me to stay in until my mom came home. So I figured I'd ask him again and see what he'd say. This time he told me to go ahead. Not knowing what was going to happen to me when I went outside. I grabbed my coat and hat, put them on and ran outside to play with one of my friends. I was so happy because my dad said I could go out. That was the last time I saw my dad, my sister, and my two brothers.

I was outside playing on a sled with my friend. I wasn't out there too long before it happened. I was run over by a bus. My friend ran into my house and told my dad. He came running outside and saw me laying in the street, limbless. I couldn't see him but my spirit could. He leaned over me, crying, calling my name. I couldn't answer him. My spirit could see the fear and the hurt in him. My dad tried wiping the blood from my nose, but it did no good. As I lay there dying, my dad just laid his hand on my chest and kept saying, "breathe baby, breathe". He kept saying it over and over again.

By now my mom was on her way home. She was coming up the hill by our house with the dinner she had bought. I think she saw the ambulance go by. She asked someone what happened. As they told her that some kid got hit by a bus up on Hawkins Street, the Holy Ghost, for those who don't understand God, right then let her know that was her son.

She started running up the hill to the house. By the time she had gotten to the house, I was already in the ambulance. They wouldn't let her in, so she went running into the house where my dad was. My dad was making all kinds of phone calls.

My mom asked him what happened. My dad told her he didn't know.

All he knew was that I was hit by a bus. My mom then asked how I looked, and if I was going to be alright. My dad told her it didn't look good at all. My dad held her as she cried.

The ambulance had already left to take me to a hospital in New Haven. My mom and dad got a ride to the hospital by our next door neighbor. On the way over to the hospital, my mom and dad prayed all the way. About half way there, my dad told my mom he felt a cold chill go through his body. He then said, "My baby's gone".

At that exact time he felt that cold chill that was the time I passed away. I had died on the way to the hospital. It was not by my choice that I leave that way, but God knows best.

Maybe God saw something even worse than death

awaiting me. No one knows but God. No God isn't a mean God. It's just that he loved me so much, he didn't want me to suffer in the long run.

Even though I was hit by a bus, I know it sounds awful, but I didn't feel any pain. It happened just that fast. I thank God for not allowing me to suffer through the accident because I hated pain.

CHAPTER EIGHT

At the hospital, it was rough on my mom. They had my parents sit and wait in this room the)/call, "the family room".

Now my dad knew deep down inside that I had already died. My mom didn't want to accept it until the doctors told her,

While they were in that room, there was a lady sitting there with a white jacket on. Dad asked her if I would be alright.

The lady wouldn't even look him in the face. She would just say, "The doctor will be in here in a few minutes." When she said that, my dad knew that I was dead. He had also seen a priest walking around outside the room they were waiting in.

My dad was trying very hard not to fall apart because he knew my mom was going to really need him.

Then, in walked the doctor. He sat down on a table next to them. He looked at my parents. At that time, my dad knew what he was going to say. He could see it in his eyes. The doctor looked at them and said, "I'm sorry, we lost him." When he said that my mom just fell apart. She just fell back in her chair and screamed. She then started crying uncontrollably.

My dad had a very hard time trying to calm her down. They stayed in that room for a long time, waiting for my mom to calm down enough to go in the room where I was laying.

After she cried for a while, my dad and family members helped my mom to the room. She wanted to see me one last time.

As she walked into the room with some help, she looked at me and said, "It looks like he's sleeping". She then leaned over me and touched me and started crying. She kept saying, "Tommy J. please open your eyes. Please open your eyes and look at mommy.

I love you Tommy J." She kept saying that while she cried over me.

My dad and some others finally got her out of the room and brought her home. She cried all the way home. She kept saying, "My Tommy J., he's gone." My dad kept holding her and telling her it was going to be alright. My dad didn't even get a chance to cry. He was trying to comfort my mom. I know how much my dad was hurting, but I also know how he wanted to be strong for my mom. Not only did he have to be strong for her, he had to go home and tell the kids what happened. The kids were going to need him also, especially Taormina. The two little ones were too young to really understand what had happened. Taormina loved me so much, that when she was told that I was dead and that she would never see me again, she didn't know what to do.

She didn't cry right away because she was in shock. They didn't really know how to react.

I don't know if she really understood at that time what death really meant. I guess after a few days, when she saw that I really wasn't coming back home, she then knew what death was.

I don't think she really cried until the day of the funeral.

The next few days after my death, my mom continued to cry. She couldn't even sleep because she was crying so much.

My dad was really worrying about her. He called the family doctor and got some medicine to help her sleep. 7ven in her sleep, she would cry. The pills did help her some, but not much. At this point, my dad still hadn't cried, or gotten any sleep. He waited to make sure my mom was going to be alright.

There were a lot of our church members at our house, as well as our family members. They all stuck by them until the funeral.

It was hard for my dad to get any sleep. He was hurting so much inside, that he was unable to cry right then. He was in his own state of shock. Everyone knew how close and how much my dad loved me. I think what hurt him the most was that I was named after him.

My dad was always a strong and brave man. He was always able to take a lot. He never showed when he was afraid, or hurting.

I have never seen my dad cry. I cried all the time.

When I got hurt. When I got mad at my mom or dad. That's why I wanted to be just like my dad. I sometimes knew when my dad was hurting, but he would cover it up by saying, "there's nothing wrong". My dad was the greatest dad in the world. He was the best.

My dad started to show his hurt when mom would call out my name in her sleep. He felt like crying, but he held back his tears and comforted my mom. Anything she wanted, my dad was right there for her. Now that's a husband. Not only a husband, that's a real dad. You don't find too many husbands and fathers like that anymore. I guess there are some.

If ever there was a time that they needed the church

that was the time. They were there on the spot whenever they even made a move. They waited on my parents hand and foot. They brought enough food to feed an army. My mom's mother came up from down south. She was very heart broken. She remembered how we had spent our vacation down there a couple of years ago.

Cur church members were there for my mom and dad night and day. Even when they got up sometimes in the morning, someone was there. That made my parents feel really good to know how much the church really cared. Tommy J., €hat was a name the whole church knew. I got along with everyone. That's one of my dad's qualities. I stole that from him. One of his many good ones.

My dad got along with everyone also.

Our family members helped my dad and mom out with the funeral arrangements. My dad is strong but he wouldn't have been able to do it alone. Our pastor was willing to help, but she didn't have to. Our pastor is the sweetest lady in the world.

She would give her last breath if it would help someone. She was my spiritual grandmother. I say that because she took my dad in as her own son. I think the hardest thing for our pastor to do was when my dad asked her to do the service. Even though my dad knew she would had done it anyway, he just had to say something to her.

We couldn't use our church for the funeral because it wasn't big enough to hold all the people that were going to be there.

The church that we did use was packed. There were no seats left.

That made my dad feel real good. That showed him how many people really loved me. I'm not just saying that, but if you had come to my funeral, you would have seen how many people were there.

The people really gave my mom and dad a lot of support.

That was good because they really needed it. There was so much love flowing through there. Pastor Moore preached at the funeral. She preached so well that many people, after the service came to her and said that they never saw or had been to a funeral like that. They said it was a beautiful funeral. There wasn't a dry eye in the church. I didn't know I had that many friends. People really cared. The songs that were sung, really moved a lot of people. I want to thank those that sang at my funeral. They really made my home going perfect. Just the way my dad wanted it. A special thanks to my pastor, and spiritual grandmother. I know it wasn't easy. I love you Pastor Moore. Promise me that you'll never forget me. I know I'll see you up in heaven. I also would like to thank each and every one of you that pitched in and helped my family. I can't call you all be name, but you know who you are. Thank you with all of my heart. After the funeral was over, and it was time to return home, it was hard. It was hard walking back into the house knowing that I wasn't walking in there with them. I know it's going to take a long time for them to get over it. I know with sod's 50 help, they will make it. They also have me rooting for them. My dad finally started to break down. It was at the funeral. He had a Reading that he had wrote and he wanted to read it himself during the service. It was very hard for him to do, but he did it. He stood up in front of the whole church and as he was reading, the tears started falling. I don't know how he did it, but I was so proud of him. You will read in this book what he wrote. It brought tears to everyone's eyes. They couldn't believe he was able to stand there and read it. It took a lot of love and courage to do that. It was so touching, even our pastor started to tear some.

My father's brother took it really hard. He really loved me. I would go to his house every Sunday before church started. He would give me and my sister anything we wanted, if he had it. He would spoil us while we were there. My mom got used to it because that's how he and my dad were brought up. My uncle is one of the nicest people you would ever want to meet. ue's funny and he's very loving. He was always a very loud person, but that was just his personality. You just had to love him. As everyone reads the reading that my dad wrote, I want you to please listen very carefully to the words. It is a very, very emotional piece of writing. I hope you will enjoy it. It may make you cry.

CHAPTER NINE

The Reading To My Mommy

To my mommy. From your Tommy J. I put this in my daddy's mind so he could write this for me, because you know I'm not here to write it myself. Daddy is writing it, but they are my words. I want you to keep this and remember, I LOVE YOU!! I love you Caddy, Mommy, Taormina, Joshy, and Bryant. Make sure, even years from now, that they remember me. Their big brother, Tommy J.

Mommy, this is your Tommy J. how I wish I could have stayed, but God had a job for me in heaven. I had to be on my way. I'm in heaven now, and God has answered all the questions I wanted to know. I asked him if I could watch over you each and every day. God told me, "yes you can son, I wouldn't have it any other way". I know it's hard for you, but daddy's there, and I want you to know, how much he really cares. He stuck not only 'by you, but by all of us. Not once did he ever really put up a fuss. I love my daddy so much and his heart, I will always touch. Ta o r m i n a and I fought all the time but that was true love and it will never die. Taormina will be smart, maybe smarter than all of us. She may not know it, but I'm going to help her. Help her through it all. I say this because you know what I mean, don't worry about school. I will help her. Taormina, you can do it, Remember, I Love You. Joshy can't understand, but someday he will. As I look down at him, I see myself. As you can see, God has put some of me in him and that you can tell. So I want you to know mommy, that when you look at Joshy, you'll be looking at me! Bryant, oh Bryant, mommy and daddy love you so. They raised you from when you were little and will never let you go. I always knew how smart you were and although you were only three years old when I died, believe me when I say, when daddy told you what happened to me, you may have been young, but you understood. That's why daddy only had to tell you once that I was in heaven and it stuck with you! Pastor Moore, my mommy and daddy love you so much. Especially my daddy, but you already know that. I still remember talking to you that day I was at your house with my daddy. He went somewhere and I stayed with you and talked your ears off. That was funny. Who knew then, that would be the bonding between you and my father. I want you to know that I love you and I will be looking over you also. Please take good care of my daddy. He told me you were my spiritual grandmother and I smiled! I have to go now. I just want to say this to my daddy. Don't blame yourself. Just remember the play you wrote, "The Chosen One", I was a chosen one. I'm in God's hands right now and I'm happy. I just want you to be, what I know God has called you to be and you know what that is. Remember I love you and always will. Mommy, after today, and it's all over with, except the fact that I'm gone, I'm gone from the house only. Not from your heart. I want you to help daddy. He's not showing it now, but he's taking it harder than everyone. He's going to need you now, more than ever. I love you mommy. Remember that you were and still are, the best mommy in the world. Please, please, stop crying. I'm home now. I'm in no pain. I'm not crying. I have a new healthy body. I still look the same. Just like you always remembered me. I'm happy. I am truly happy! Bye Mommy. Bye Daddy. Bye Taormina. Bye Joshy. Bye Bryant. I will see all of you again one day. Right now, your-lives must go on! Remember, I will always, always be withyou forever (in your hearts). Remember Me, (Tommy J.) I hope that everyone that reads this reading, will get something out of it. It wasn't meant just for my family. It was meant for families all over the world. There are little kids like myself dying all over the world everyday. This isn't meant to scare anyone. It is meant to make you think. What if this happened to your little child? I'm not trying to speak anything on anyone's family, but what if it was your child. I know it put my family through a lot of pain, but it also made them stronger. Would you be able to deal with the situation? Cr would you let the situation deal with you. Death doesn't come easy, but it does come. (The day, it will come to your family. Will you be able to stand? Or will you fall? This reading was meant to strengthen those who have already lost a young loved one, and to encourage those in the future, to continue to stand. For one day, one of your kids may write, or inspire someone in your family to write something similar to this. I told you it was enough to make you cry. If you didn't, I know you felt like it. So parents, be strong, especially the mothers.

CHAPTER TEN

HOW TO COPE AND DEAL WITH THE DEATH OF A YOUNG LOVED ONE

Hi, I'm Tommy J.'s father. This isn't easy for me to do, but I just want to talk about death a little. Also, how to cope with death. Not only coping with it, but dealing with it. Especially when it's a young family member. To some people, death comes easy to them. I don't know if it is because they don't really have deep feelings for that person, or their love has waxed cold. When I say waxed cold, I mean that maybe some people have been through so much hurt and Pain that it is hard for them to show their true feelings. It's your child, I don't care you through, they are still yours.

More than enough to break you up. He allows you to have children so Vr of them. Not half raise them, them. I feel that if a child some reason, they run into some f they're not strung out on drugs, one home. A parent that can say,

"Son (daughter), remember that you always have a room here", are very loving parents. Remember, they are yours.

For a parent to lose a child and not even weep over them, that is just cold. Even Jesus wept. The same compassion Jesus had God put in us as parents. So those parents whose love has waxed cold toward their children, stop it! Bad enough that you lost your child, but does that child still have to fight for your love even after he/she is gone?

Just seeing them laying there breathless, should bring the walls down. After the walls come down, a'sk God to forgive you for your coldness. Ask God to restore the love and compassion you had when they were first born. It's still there, you just need God in your life. He will restore that which you have lost. He will remind you that, that was your own flesh and blood. Yes, you'll feel guilty and ashamed of yourself. You ought to be. I feel that the worse thing a parent can do, is not love their own child.

To most people, death comes hard to them. The main reason I feel is because they don't expect it. When it comes by surprise, it catches you off guard. You don't know how to react.

You don't know what to do. Some people can't even cry right away. They go into shock. These are only natural reactions.

My son's death took me by surprise. I was in the house with my son up until I told him he could go outside. It seemed like a few minutes later, he was dead. As I ran outside and saw him lying there, limbless, my heart almost stopped. As I saw that there was nothing I could do to help him, a part of me was dying right along with him. As the b1 was running out of his body, if felt like my blood was running nut of my body, I wished it was me laying there instead of my son. I would have given anything to switch places with him. I told Gtid to take me instead of my son.

I didn't know what to do. My son was dying, and there wasn't a thing I could do. As the ambulance took him away, I waited for my wife to return home. She was on her way. She came running in the house with a look of fear on her face. I knew that she heard it was our son that was hit. She asked me how he was and if he was going to be alright. I was already in shock and it was very hard for me to look at her and tell her the truth. It took everything in me to tell her it didn't look good at all.

I grabbed her and held her as she really started crying.

We held each other for a little while before we realized that we needed a ride to the hospital. (your next door neighbor was nice enough to give us a ride. A lot of things go through your mind when something like this happens. That ride to the hospital is the longest ride in a parent's life. A5 we were on the way there, my wife and I started praying. We asked God to please save our son. We were binding the death angle, but it was to late. We were about half way there, when I felt a cold chill go through my whole body. At that time, I looked at my wife and said, "he's gone". I told her a cold chill went through my boay. Needless to say, as you read in the book, our son died.

There's no worse feeling in the world that!, that of losing a child.

We didn't think about taking our own life, but we did wonder how we could enjoy the rest of our lives without him;

My wife was totally out of it for two or three days. She couldn't sleep or eat. As she laid in bed crying, she tried to get some sleep. Even with the medicine I got for her, she still tossed and turned. I cried in my spirit as I watched her. I wanted to help her, but all I could do was sit and hold her.

In a situation like that, I think the only thing a husband can do is try to comfort his wife. After a few days, sheiyies able to stop crying for a while.

She didn't want anyone to take our kids to their house because she needed to see them. She needed to be able to holl them.

I feel they made coping with our son's death a little easier.

I did all that I could, but just being able to hug the kids gave it that little extra added touch. I feel that somehow, my wife gained some strength from our kids. It can be very helpful when you have more than child. The love that flows from your children can pick you

After a couple of days, my up. wife was able to talk to some of our church members and our family members. The prayers of the saints truly did held us up. The love of our family members helped us a lot. My wife couldn't wait for mother to arrive.

When she did, that really lifted her. My wife really loves her mother, as all children should. The one thing my wife held on to other than our kids was, God! She refused to get angry with God. Without Christ in her life, I would hate to think what might have been going through her mind.

My wife is a lot stronger than I thought she was. Under the circumstances, I feel she did very well. Although I was really hurting inside, I was glad to see that she was finally coming around. God had given her some new strength. He allowed her to cry until she couldn't cry anymore. After the tears, she was even able to eat some food. Not much, but she, did eat.

On the other hand, I was having a hard time dealing with my son's death. After holding him and seeing that there was nothing I could do, that was hurt beyond what I could explain. My wife couldn't see what I was going through because she was hurting.

I was trying hard to be strong. I felt my family really needed me and I had to put my feelings on hold until I was able to comfort them. I was brought up in a family where the men had to be tough. In some situations it works, but this wasn't one of them.

I feel it hurt me more by not letting it all out when it hanicenel.

I held it in so long, it had to come out sooner or later. I was hurting because I lost my son. Not only that, I think a father hurts even more if his son is named after him. There's just something about losing I was trying to cope and deal with everything in a manly way.

I was trying to lick my wounds and be strong as well. You know what? I found out the best way for me „being a man, was to turn to God. As my wife held on to God, so did I. I had so much anger in me, I had to let it out. It seemed as though I was mad at everyone. The one person I couldn't take my anger out on was God.

Even when God took my son home to be with him, I still couldn't get angry with God.

After the dudt had settled, I spoke with my pastor and she said that she knows how much we loved Tommy J. It's just that God loved him more. I then thought about how God must have seen what awaited my son and wanted to stare him from it. I then thought, "Well God, if you had to take my son, why did it have to be in that way?" Then it dawned on me that if it hadn't been this way, what awaited him may have been even worse. This really has strengthened us. This would either make you strong, or it would completely destroy you. Through it all, I still managed to hold on to God. Most people probably would have turned their back on God, but not me. It made me want to serve him even more.

God is a good God and I will continue to serve him. I get joy through serving him.

I was bitter for a while, but God removed the bitterness from my heart. I was so angry at the driver that hit my son.

I didn't think I could control my temper. Through God, and the prayers of the saints, I was able to pull myself together.

Through the prayer of my pastor, and the saints, I was able to rest easy. I thank God for Pastor Moore, She treats me as though I was her own son. I know that no one else was praying for us, she was. If I could steal her, I would. She has been a great help to us. I know, the hardest thing for her to do for us was the funeral service. She loved Tommy J., and I know it was hard for her.

Pastor Moore and I have grown pretty close over the years, and she even lets me call her, "Ma". I just want to take this time out to thank her personally. Ma, I want you to know how much I appreciate all you have done for us in-our time of sorrow. I know we can't pay you for the love you have shown us. I felt by writing about your love in this book, it would really be the best way of saying, "thanks". You know how much we love you an we always will. Remember, your stuck with me. 'whether you like it or not (smile).

Just talking to my pastor was a big help. I needed someone with a listening ear, and someone with enough wisdom and knowledge to counsel me. Yes, I talk very highly of my pastor because there's none better. Just being around her or even talking to her on the phone, I was able to draw some of her strength.

It felt like I was draining, but I know she didn't mind.

I feel it would be easier to deal with your own death that is if you knew you were dying, than it is dealing with the loss of your own child. For one reason, you would be able to pull yourself together before easing your way into telling your loved ones. Secondly, you can pick the right time to tell them. It's as though the ball is in your court, so to speak. Third, that would also give you enough time to get things in order, and to prepare for it. Although no one wants to prepare for their own death.

I know I don't want to.

When someone knocks on your door and says your son or daughter was just hit by a bus, that's a total shock. When you open your door, that's the last thing you expect them to tell you. When and if it ever happens to anyone other than us, I hope this book will be able to help you. I want, our experience with death not to be your experience with death. We all know death will come knocking at the door of your home sooner or later. I feel that sharing this with you will be a big help to you. I pray that everyone that reads this book, will be blessed by this book.

Though the road looks rough, remember hold on to God. You must hold on to sod. If not, the devil will take everything from you.

It took some time before I was able to really believe it happened. Even though the funeral was over with, and I was back home. Still in my head, I kept saying, "I can't believe it. I can't believe it." I thought it was a nightmare and I couldn't wake up. In time, it's going to take time, I was able to deal with it. With God's help, I still think about it, and my heart starts to beat a little fast. I manage to calm myself down. my wife has finally started to feel a little better. She's just glad that our son is up in heaven.

No parent wants their child to die before them. I know we didn't. We as parents, bring them into this world that they may have a full life. I felt that if someone died at a young age, that they were dealt a bad hand. It seemed like life was like a poker game. If you were dealt a tough hand, and you didn't know what to do, you had at least three options:

(1) You could fold, meaning you could either stop fighting and just give up on life. or

(2) You could bluff, meaning you could go through life screaming and cheating people. Never letting people see the real you. Always being mysterious and faking everything. or

(3) You can play it straight, meaning you can live life to the fullest.

By being honest, straight forward, and by letting God lead you in the right direction, you play it straight. For we all need some direction in our lives and who better to lead the way life was a poker game, I would bet on God. He's a sure thing.

I guess one of the hardest things for us to deal with is not being able to watch our son grow up with the other kids in the house. It's taking some time for us to get use too. With the help of God, I know we'll be able to deal with his absence.

We find it hard because we were so used to seeing our Tommy J. running around the house. If he wasn't getting into one thing, he was getting into another. We didn't realize how much we missed it, until he was gone. The house just wasn't the same anymore. There was such a quietness in the house. I really do miss him.

To m m y J. was the type of kid that would play with everyone in the house. Be didn't just play with this one today, and that one tomorrow. His presence was always known. Tommy J. was probably the happiest kid I have ever seen. He kept Taormina, Joshy, and Bryant going. I know they really miss him a lot.

I would have to tell him to stop messing with Joshy and Bryant sometimes. Not because he was playing too much. I realize that was just his way of showing how much he loved them. I would give just about anything if I could tell Tommy. J. to leave them alone right now. I know that I can't. Tommy J. was such a loving son, and me being his father, that's why I find it so har to get over him. One day you're telling him to stop it, and then the next day, you're unable to say anything to him because he's not there. You even go and look in his bedroom, but ho one is in there. You look at his bed, and the tears start to run down your cheek. There is no worse feeling than that of losing a loved one and then looking at the bed in which they were supposed to be laying in. I'm telling you now, it really hurts.

Not only that, one of the things I find myself doing is, I don't know if my wife does it or not but I find myself calling my other son's Tommy J. by mistake. I really don't mean to do it but that lets me know that I'm still not over his death yet.

Until I can stop calling my son's Tommy J., I will never get over it. I don't want to forget Tommy J., and I know I never will.

I just want to get over him. Some may say that sounds harsh, but if you don't let i-41. go, it will either drive you into an early grave, or into the nut house. With the Lord's help, I chose to let it go and so did my wife. I'm not going to tell you it's easy because it's not. I am not completely over it, but I have been able to deal with it. The best way to do that is, just take it one day at a time. After a while, you'll see that your life has slowly moved ahead. 7verythilkg didn't come to a stop and stay there. As we all know, life must go on. With or without our loved ones. For we can do all things through Christ, who strengthens us, and God has done it.

I noticed that this incident has really done something my wife in a positive way. As well as myself, it has drawn us closer to our other children. I've seen how my wife use to be pretty free with the kids. Meaning she could let the kids play in one half of the house for hours and not have to worry about them. Now I notice how she goes in the same end of the house that the kids are playing in. It's like she has to be near them.

I don't see that as a problem. As a matter of fact, I love seeing how close she has gotten to the kids.

I find myself even closer to my kids now than I ever was.

Not that we weren't close or that 1 didn't love my kids. It's just that I was working so hard, I really didn't get the chance to spend as much time with them as I would have liked too. Now I find myself playing with my kids at home. We roll all around on the floor. I carry Joshy and Bryant on my shoulders. I let them jump all over me 'band punch on me. They love that.(smile)

I am really starting to enjoy my kids. I see that they are much happier when I spend some time with them everyday. I really try to make time for them, they're worth it.

I know I didn't spend too much time with my daughter, but I want you to know, it wasn't because I didn't love her. I guess it was because she was a girl and I figured she would hang out with her mother and the boys would hang out with me. I know that was a bad excuse. Now I look back and I feel so bad about the way I treated her.

After Tommy J. died, I did become pretty close with my daughter.

We began by talking to one another a lot more. We would watch movies together and regular television shows. I even let' my daughter help me prepare some meals for dinner. My wife had taught her how to cook a little. I really couldn't think of what to do with her because it had been so long. My wife has said, why don't I take Taormina to the basketball game with me. I said that she wouldn't like it. My wife asked, "How do you know unless you ask her?" I did ask her and she said she wanted to go, so I took her with me. Do you know what? She really enjoyed it. It was hard for me because I know that I would have taken

To m m y J., but I can truly say that I really enjoyed having her along. It was strange, but it was nice. I plan to take Taormina to a lot more sporting events with me if she wants to go. She can fill in the gap until Joshy and Bryant get a little older.

By then, Taormina will be older and she may find other interests.

For now., I'm going to try and make every moment count. Time is very precious. I found that out the hard way. I also found out that the one I spent the least amount of time with, was the one that was just like me.

Ta o r m i n a is like me in many ways. She acts like me. She also changes her moods like me. When I look at her today, I see she's growing up almost in the same way I did. That's what I don't want her to do. I realize how hard I am on her. Not for the wrong reasons, but because she's a girl. I feel a father has to be tougher on his daughter than on his son because later in life, the girl has to deal with the cunningness of men. I'm tough on her now, but she'll thank me in years to come. I love my daughter. I know I don't tell her as much as I should so, this is another way for me to show her how much I love her.

To m m y J. said that she will be very smart, and I believe it.

She has really improved in school and I'm looking for her to go a long, long way. She can do it if she really wants too. Curing this crisis, my daughter has been very brave. Not only that, she has been a big help to myself as well as to my wife.

My wife looked to our daughter for many things. That also brought them closer.

My wife really got close to Joshy and Bryant, and I loved it.

She started reading to them at night before they went to bed.

She spoiled them a little by bringing them work. She would run all through the house something home from chasing them and laughing with them. The things she use to do with Tommy J., she now does it with them. I get a charge of excitement whenever I see them happy. That should have been Tommy J.'s middle name.

He always had a smile on his face. When he died, he didn't look bad at all. He looked at peace. If there was anything I could or anyone else could say about Tommy J., they would say he, was always happy and that he really loved his family.

I sometimes sit back and look at my family and I see the closeness this incident has brought them. I thank God for my family. I may be minus one, but I can still enjoy the family I have left. God is really doing something special in my household.

Any parent that goes through something like this, it will make you very protective of your other children. I mean very protective—My wife and I find it very hard for us to let our kids out of our sight. Many people have said they would take the kids off our hands for a while but we are unable to let them go. That over protectiveness had set in. We knew they meant well, it's just that a feeling of fear for your other kids comes upon you. Even though we knew that was just what we needed, we just couldn't let them get away from us. I feel that's a natural reaction.

I can truly say that I became very, very protective.

Whenever my wife and kids were gone form the house too long, I started to panic. I recall a time when my wife took the kids down to the store. It wasn't too far from the house, but they had walked.

I felt that it shouldn't have taken them as long as it did.

After about 20-25 minutes, I got up, put my shoes on and started out the door. I still was not at ease yet and as I stepped out our door, they had come around the aide of the house. My wife looked at me like, "I know you weren't coming to look for us".

I told her yes, I was. I told her I was getting nervous because she was taking too long. She looked at me and saw that I was serious. She said that she wasn't gone long at all. 7o you know what? She wasn't gone that long. The twenty minutes they were gone, felt like hours. That goes to show you how protective I had become. My wife and kids had gotten out of the house for a little while and here I was ready to go out searching for them. I knew it was going to take some time, but I didn't know it was going to be that hard. I knew deep down inside that they were alright, but the devil kept telling me that something was wrong.

When you are going through a hard time, especially when you have just lost a loved one, the devil likes to try and play mind games on you. He will tell you another bad disaster has occurred.

You, being weak and feeling your worse, can easily believe what the devil is ministering to you. The best thing I could do after I had left my house to look for my family, was to from that day on, trust and believe in God. It was hard for me to give them some breathing room. It is taking my wife just as long as it is taking me. She really found it hard to slack off.

Sometimes it can hurt your children if you smoother

them. It's alright to protect your family, but I found out it hurts the kids if you over protect them.

I noticed how the kids were much more active after I eased up on protecting them. I started letting my daughter spend nights over her girlfriends houses. For a while, I would tell her that her friends had to come stay at our house. My wife said that wasn't right. If they could come and stay at our house, then Taormina should be allowed to stay over their houses finally gave in, and it made our daughter much happier.

It did my heart good to finally let my wife go. I wanted to keep her at home so I would always know where she was. That would have done more harm to our marriage than good. We always had a good marriage, but when I gave my wife some room to move, our relationship got stronger.

I can honestly say, a time will come when both husband and wife will begin to dig into each other, meaning they will get on each other's nerves. I guess it took about five months after our son's death, before we had our first big fight. Not with hands, but with words. I want to tell you, words can sometimes hurt more than actually fighting with your hands. We began to say things to one another that we really didn't mean. At that time, we were hurting each other's feelings. Feelings can be shattered very easily, and sometimes they can take a might long time to put them back together again.

I thank God that neither one of us had come out and accused one another of our sons death. It was hard for us to understand but we didn't point the finger. You will be surprised at all the things you can find to pick a fight with your spouse. Then, after you are finished fighting, you will start to think about it and you'll realize that it was very silly. If there are any husbands like me, you will stay mad at your wife for days. The thing about it, you will come around. You have to remember, yo1.1 can't stay mad forever. You can try, I know I have, but it 1:esn't work. God will never allow it.

I found out that in your time of sorrow, you have to let out a release. It's not intended for anyone, but you can't hold it in or it'll get worse. It's always best to get it off your chest.

After you let it out, then you can try to put the pieces together.

It won't be easy, but it can be done. God has a handle on everything. If you allow things to get out of hand and go too far, you can begin to hate one another. That isn't God's will.

God's will is that we prosper, and be in health, even as our soul prospers. Before that can take place, the husband and wife must work things out.

I, like most men, am an easy person. However, I can work up a temper, just like most men, if I'm pushed a little too far. I really hate getting angry. So instead of going off on my spouse, I would leave the house and return when I felt that things had calmed down. Absence sometimes makes the heart grow fonder. The feelings of losing Tommy J. had begun to surface again when his birthday came around. It was very hard for us to deal with that because we weren't able to see him enjoy it.

To m m y J. always had fun on his birthday. Not being able to celebrate it can be very, very gad. It's hard because all our kids are young, and it seems strange celebrating their birthdays and not Tommy J.'s. Tommy J. was full of so much joy when he knew his birthday was coming. I feel bad because if he had lived, I was going to give him a surprise birthday party. He would have been eight years old, and it would had been his very first. I miss my Tommy J. so much. I still kiss his picture everyday.

I know he's gone, but fathers, you will probably do the same think.

It helps me somehow make it through the day. It may sound strange but you'll know what I mean.

Birthdays are very special to little kids. They know it comes only once a year, so they try to get everything they possibly can. I always tried to get Tommy J. just what he wanted but even if I couldn't, he was always understanding. That's what I love and miss about him. If I didn't get it for him the, he knew I would get it for him later. I am going to make it my business to visit his grave every year on his birthday. I don't care how hard it may be, I at least owe him that much. He was my heart.

I will never ever forget Tommy J.

The main thing I have learned through this whole incident was to hold onto God no matter what. Parents can very easily blame God for a fatal death in the family and give up on the one that has created us. I hope that one day if anyone goes through this, that the story that has been told in this book, will be a big help to them. I found God to be a friend when I felt like I was all alone. I found God to be a healer, because my heart was broken. I found God to be a comforter, for I became very restless. I found God to be all that I have needed in my time of sorrow.

God can and God will make everything alright. God is a good God. God is good all the time. No one can make me doubt him because I know too much about him. No one knows like I know, what the lord has done for me. God had brought me from a mighty long way, where of I am glad.

I would have given anything at the moment of my son's death to have traded places with him. It happened not, so today and every day, I thank God for being among the living.

I pray that the story of my son's life and death, will be a help to someone.

I also pray that everyone help to make this book a big success.

Not for me, but for my son Tommy J. I know he would want everyone to know about him. He was a very, very, very, special young man.

I thank God for my family and how he has kept us together through it all. I thank God for strengthening my family even the more. I pray that God will bless everyone that reads this book.

I thank God for the saints of God, and for all the help they have given us, and all the prayers that went up for us.

I thank God for my Pastor in a mighty special way. For she has treated me just like a son from day one. She had been a big help to me and my family. God had truly blessed me with a beautiful Pastor, he has also blessed me with a very dear friend. I love Pastor Wiola Moore just like a mother. I know she keeps me and my family in her prayers.

Most of all, I thank God for giving me the strength to write this book. I know it was God and not me. I pray that God will complete his work in me, for I belong to him. For God I live and for God die. Again, I pray that everyone help to make this book a big success. Remember, this book is in memory of our son

To m m y J. (We love you Tommy J.) May God Bless Everyone!!!

THE END

GETTING PAST "THE HUM"
"MY LIFE" BEFORE "MY DEATH"
AT SEVEN YEARS OLD.
Written By: Thomas B. Green, Sr
Inspired By: Thomas B. Green, Jr.

This book is a continuation of the book "My Life, before "My Death" at (7) seven years old. This story picks up with tommy J.'s father telling how one must go on with their life and get past the hurt. it may sound easier than it actual5is, but it isn't.

Some people are able to pull themselves together and go on, and there are some people that never get, pastihe hurt, and never put their lives back together.

This story is told from Tommy J's father's point of view, and his life experience. Please help make this book a success.

This book is written in Loving Memory of our son, (Tommy J.), we still love you.

CHAPTER ELEVEN

My name is Thomas Green Sr., and this book is about Getting Past The Hurt, and going on with your life. I am writing this because, in my first segment, I wrote about the tragic loss of my seven year old son, Tommy J. he of course was named after me. And when he died, that really did something to me, it brought on a hurt that you wouldn't believe.

I was only thirty years old when I lost my son. To me that's very young, and very hard for any person. My wife was only twenty-eight years old, so you can imagine how hard it was for her, and the hurt that she felt. We just a young married couple trying to raise our family the best we knew how. We were married five years when the incident happened.

I can honestly say that we hall a solid foundation. Our kids were very, very happy. But when the incident happened it shook up our whole family. Yes I know everyone will say that's normal under those conditions. So, what I am trying to say is, even though it may seem normal, it sometimes breaks up families. It can become so hurtful that the spouses can't take it and end up going their own separate ways. And the ones that really get hurt, are the remaining children if there area any. In which I think most families do have more than one child. I'm not saying all this to tell you that my wife and I separated, because we didn't, we're still together.

I said all that to say, when there's death in the family, that's the time you have to stick together. You have to remember, mommy and daddy aren't the only ones that have to get pass the hurt. If you would just look down you'll see that the children also must get past he hurt. Kids are people too, they hurt just like we do.

I also found out that the kids sometimes hurt more than the parents.

I know someone is saying how that can be. Well, I'll tell you I found it to be true because, if you think about it, most kids in their up growing share a room and that brings a closeness between them that parents don't realize. They become more than just brothers and sisters, they become best friends. Some people may now be saying how do I know.

I know firsthand because when my son Tommy J. died, I seen the change in my kids. I saw the hurt in my oldest child's eyes, which is my daughter. I know she's hurting because I see her when she just walks around the house. I know deep down inside her, that he was her best friend. I know my daughter, and I knew my son gm very well. She misses him very much. I see the loneliness in my son'

Bryant. I feel that he misses him most. I'm not saying that we didn't love Tommy J. as much as he did, because we did. It's just that, Bryant slept in the same room with Tommy J. and they talked all night until they fell asleep. I know because I could hear them. Bryant and Tommy J. probably shared funny moments that we don't even know about. You could just tell by the happy laughter that came from their bedroom.

There are times when Bryant tells me that he misses Tommy J. I mean this is coming from a little four year old boy. He would say it on his own. I walked in Bryant's room day just to see what he was doing and I sat down on the bed and started thinking about Tommy J., Bryant came over to me and said, I miss Tommy J. too. That's how smart and sensitive Bryant is. He can't fully express his feelings but, I know how much he really misses his brother Joshua was very young when it happened but, I can't say that he didn't know his brother. I know that he knew him and loved him.

Every day I bring Joshua into our living room and tell him to look up on the wall and tell me whose picture he sees. He looks up and says, that's Tommy J. I do that because him being so young, it would be easy for him to forget his brother. I am going to see that he doesn't. I want Joshua to always remember his big brother, and how much we all loved him.

Kids, they are much too precious to ignore during a crisis. it wouldn't take much for them to crawl into a shell and never come out. That's why I'm urging every family that is going through a crisis, to please stick together. If not for your sakes, do it for the kid's sake. You will be surprised how your child can hold you up.

I can say that because, after Tommy J.'s funeral, I thought that was it for me. I had lost my oldest son who was only seven, and I didn't think I could make it without him. No I didn't contemplate suicide. It's just that Tommy J. reminded me so much of myself, that I couldn't bargit. I wouldn't wish the hurt and pain I went through on anybody. Death doesn't come easy to anyone.

(1)

I didn't know what to do, or even how I was going to go on. This has taken me totally by surprise. And then you ask yourself, what am I going to do now? I had so many plans for us. And now, now they're all gone. All my hopes and dreams for Tommy J have vanished.

I'm saying, most parents already had a dream or a vision of what they see their children as (20) twenty years down the line. I see Tommy J. as a money maker. I see him being a very rich business man. Why, because he was always able to keep money. Even when mommy and daddy didn't have any, we could always go to Tommy J. and borrow some. Someone may be asking, how and where he got money from. Tommy J. Would get four and sometimes five dollars a week for his allowance, and then there were some good friends and some family members that would also give him some money.

What Tommy J. would do is he would take maybe one dollar of his money and spend it. The rest of his money, he would go in his bedroom and hide it. Taormina would end up spending all her allowance then try to talk (Tommy J. into spending his money on her. But he was too smart for that. He would tell her no, and that nobody told her to spend her money.

And just when my wife and I were out of money, and we needed to get a few things in the house to eat. We would say that we don't h ave any money to get anything and Tomnmy J. would say, I got some money. We would look at him and say, we don't need any change, we need dollars. And he'd tell us that's what he's got. We'd look at him, and just to humor him we'd tell him to go get it. By now we're thinking he was going to come back with about fifty cents.

And to our surprise, he came back with dollar bills more than enough for us to get some food in the house. When I asked him where he got so much money from, he said, I saved my allowance.

Right then I knew we have us a rich business man in the future.

But, Tommy J. was always amazed with cops. He loved to watch cop show on T.V. So, although I salami son as a rich business man, deep down inside, I believe he wanted to a rich police officer. I sit back and think sometimes, I wonder what Tommy J. would have been. Now I'll never know. That's why I'm writing this book, because it is helping me to get past the hurt. It's not easy, but I know with God's help, I will get past the hurt, me as well as my family. We are in this together. God said that he would see us through, and he kept his word. God's word is one thing we can always depend on.

My family and I were suffering to survive. I am saying, we all were suffering a great deal, but we all had to survive. An ordeal that has destroyed many families. Death, that's one word that can destroy even the closest knit family.

(3)

My biggest problem to deal with was seeing how much my family was suffering) I too was suffering but, there was no time for the pain, I had a family to take care of. My family needed me and I had to hold myself together long enough to make sure they had survived.

Although I was just barely surviving myself.

The pain I was feeling, I had held inside for a long time. As a matter of fact, I am still till this day, holding in a lot of pain.

I haven't been able to release all the hurt and pain that I'm holding in. I don't know why, but, I do know that the only way for me to turn that page in my life is to let out a good release. I mean I have to bring myself to really cry. It has been almost (one year) at the time I wrote this part and I still haven't cried like I want too.

I realize that there is a healing process and that I have to go through it. I just pray that God will help me to release all the hurt, pain, and yes, hatred. When I say hatred, I mean, I hate the fact that my son is dead, and I still see the man that killed my son, driving the bus. It takes everything in me not to approach him and tell him what I really think about him. It's like he just went on with his life as though he never hit and killed a little seven year old boy. A boy who was so full of life. A boy who had everything to live for.

As time went by, I started feeling very depressed. I felt myself moping around, even at my job. I wasn't loosing my mind or anything, it's just that it felt like I was in my own little world. I knew what was going on around me butiI wanted in a way, to be by myself felt like I needed to hide away, just get away from it all.

The walls were closing in on me. It was as though I couldn't breath, I needed some air. At times, even now, I want to get in my car and get away for a few days.

My wife and kids went away for two weeks to see her mother down south. Even though I had the house to myself, it's not the same as getting away for awhile. And I feel that's what I need more than anything. Not because I want to get away from my wife and kids, but because I need some time by myself so I can really say good-bye to Tommy J. I love my wife and kids but I need to dot this. I want to be able to finally put Tommy J. to rest. And by doing so, I can finally put my mind at ease. My mind and my heart are weighing very heavy right now, I need some relief I'm not trying to hide from people, I just need some time alone. I know it's impossible for me to run and hide forever, because I have to many responsibilities to take care of. Sometimes I feel like, if I could, I would. My wife and kids papaptitxbtkpar sometimes gigic call me, "Mr. be by yourself." I don't tell her, but, that's how I really feel at times.

There are times when I see that bus driver coming past me and I just want to let out a scream. I know sooner or later I'll get some time to myself. I know they say it's not good to want to be by yourself after such a great loss. For those who want to know why, the reason is, while you are going through your depression, the devil can, and will try to play tricks on your mind. His job is to steal, to kill and destroy. The develeftwill first try to steal your mind, then he will kill any feelings that you have, then he will try and make you feel like th ere's nobody by your side, and t hat there is nothing left for you to live for. And that is when he will try to destroy you.

Whoever is going through some similar pain and hurt, don't give in.

Remember, it doesn't help anything by running away. Because after you finish running you sit down to try and relax, you can rest assure t hat the problem you were running away from will be sitting right on your shoulders.

CHAPTER TWELVE

There are times when I close my eyes just for a moment and I have flashbacks about what happened. I hate to dwell on the incident because I can get caught up in the whole ordeal again. When that happens, I have to snap out of it.

To me there is nothing worse than having a nightmare about someone dear you have loss. When I say nightmare, I mean when you relive what happened, but this time the devil makes you see it in a more disgusting and more painful way. You begin to see more damage done to you child and more blood everywhere.

That is enough to make you go for some professional help. It will also make you not want to go* to sleep. Because most people believe that dreams come true. What am I talking about!!!! I am saying that some people feel that a dream like that means more death. And that puts even more fear into that family.

But I'm here to tell you that God can remove that fear and give you peace of mind. God can ease the pain and mend the broken heart.

God can do for you what man could never do. I know it takes time to get over certain things, but God can help you get through it a lot easier.

Yo u know what I found hard, but I found it also to be very true!!!

It's that, nothing lasts forever. Cars don't, houses don't, money don't, food don't, clothes don't, and most of all people don't. No I'm not trying to compare people or life to the things that I have just mentioned.

It's just that down here on earth, these are material things and they come and go. One year you have it, one year you don't, one month you have it, one month you don't, one day you have it, one day don't. These things don't and won't last forever. Some of you are probably saying, what are you talking about?

Well, what I am saying is, that God has placed all of us down here on earth for an appointed time. And that our lives here won't last forever. Sooner or later we will depart from here. And as for our children, it was God's will for men and women to be fruitful and multiply. Meaning, God intended for us to have children, and to raise them as best we know how. But, we must also look at it as, we are all God's children, we belong to him. And when death comes to your home for one of your children, no matter how old or how young. Just try to look at it this way — God let us borrow him or her for the time that you did have them. It was just time for them to go back to their father's house which is in heaven.

I know it sounds easier said than done but I say this from experience. it helped me in getting past the hurt. Just knowing that he's in God's hands and that he is in a better place. Most of all, thank God or allowing you to have him or her for that time.

My son slipped away, but how better to slip to thank God himself.

I also found that, to get past the hurt, you must first get past the emotions. (Emotions) meaning your feelings, your thoughts, and your reactions. All these things must be dealt with, then you 0n start to move on with your life. Yes you still have a life!!!!

Most people that suffer a great loss have a very hard time putting behind them, I know I did. I found it hard to do even over a year later. some things are just to hard to shake. Death, you never forget it, but you must get past it.

I often look at other families and how their world is so full of joy and then I look at how my world has been turned up side down.

I'll see a family with a son that looks like he's seven or eight years old and right away my mind starts thinking about my son. At that moment I go with that feeling for a little while, then I have to pull myself in because I don't like to dwell on it to long.

I'm not saying it's wrong to think in the past, but I am saying be careful not to get caught up in it. Why? because all you'll be doing is putting yourself through all that pain again.

You know what, I've learned through experience that behind every dark cloud, there is a ray of light. And as you go through your hurt, pain and suffering that ray of light gets brighter and brighter. What am I talking about it's just like, when the sun goes down, every thing is dark and can't see your way.

But when the sun begins to rise, and that ray of light comes shining through, then you are able to see your way. Meaning, after loosing someone, your life may seem very dark. You don't know what your going to do, how your going to make it, or if you want to make it. Listen, even you have a ray of light ready to shine through all that darkness. I always say if I could make it, so can you.

My life is slowly being put back together by God!!!

I asked god to put my life back together and that's what he's doing. It's being done slowly because there's a healing process I must go through and so will you. I'm positive that I'll be just fine, and if you let God do it for you, I'm positive you'll be just fine also.

After some time has passed I started going over my brother's house. It was hard for me at first because he has kids and one of them is a boy. At first it was hard watching him run around playing because I'd ask God why me, why my son, as if I hadn't asked that question a thousand times already. Eventually I got pass that stage and again I thank God for that because 'I love my nephew.

I would like to take a moment to tell everyone about a lady who helped me through my darkest times. She may not know it but she helped me more th an she could ever imagine. Her name is Pastor Viola Moore, but she lets me call her Malt! She knew when my son was weighing heavy on my mind and she would say to me remember, I'm praying for you. Just when I needed to be comforted she would say something to me.

There were many times I would call her up just to hear her voice, but she knew what I needed and she would pray for me on the phone.

There was something about her voice that was very soothing. After I would get off the phone with Mal! It was as if a heavy load was lifted off my shoulders. I love my Pastor very much and she knows it.

The way death comes is never pleasant. Some people plan for their own deaths. What I mean by that is, some are told by their doctors that they only have a certain amount of months to live. I know that's a hard pill to swallow but that also gives you same time to prepare for it.

I myself know that only God can prolong death - If you truly believe in God, he can add years onto your life.

Death also comes unexpected. I can honestly say that my son's death was unexpected. I say this because there are many other families who have lost a family member unexpectedly. Death can come loudly, by way of fighting and screaming or it can also come the way many people are dying today, that way being by guns. Death also comes without a sound. What I mean by that is, there are many people that die in their sleep. You also have people, that take their own lives, which isn't right, but they think they're taking the easy way out by taking an overdose of pills.

They take a hand full of pills and when they fall asleep, that's it, and it's all over. But I'm here to tell you that God is not pleased with anyone that takes their own life. For one of God's commandments was, (THOU SHALT NOT KILL). So killing yourself will only give you a one way ticket to (HELL), so think before you act.

Where do you want to spend eternity? Heaven or Hell. I'm living to make it into Heaven, I want to see Jesus' face to face.

I thank God for my Pastor and the family. I took my son's death very hard, and I'll tell you, it became somewhat easier just being around them. I want too personally thank Elliott Moore. I know he probably want to know why!! It's not so much that he had all the comforting words. It's just that, whenever he needed a ride somewhere, I was more than glad to do it. Just by giving Elliott a ride, I had someone with me, and I had someone to talk too. But most of all, Elliott helped me to keep my mind off of death, and onto life. For that Elliott, I personally thank you (one more thing Elliott, don't think you're getting some money from me because I mentioned you in my book, "NO" I'm just kidding).

It also helps if you can find something or remember something that will make you laugh and smile. I found that's one thing that can't hurt you, it only helps I want to take the time to mention my godson, his name is Justin.

I have to tell you, being his godfather has made my life a little more cheerful. Yes I still have children of my own, and no I'm not putting my godson before them. At one of my lowest points in my life, Justin was able to restore some joy in life.

I want to say, there's nothing like having your own children. And I Love my children very much. I learn more and more from my children every day. And two years later God has blessed my wife and I with another child. And get this, the due date is Thanksgiving Day. Believe, me, when you have lost a child, and then God turns around and blesses us with a newborn, that is something to be thankful about.

The last thing I would like to talk about is, how your friends can sometimes hurt you. Even your best friends. I found out through my own experience that your friends mean well, but they tend to stop coming around you much too soon. I feel that they don't quite understand that you need them to be around until you start healing some. Losing my son was the worst thing that ever happened to me. And when I needed my friends to be around me the most, they weren't there. It felt as though I was all by myself. I thank God I was able to lean on him. With God's help and strength, I was able to make it through that rough time in my life.

In the closing of this story, I asked that if you have read this book Anyone that has lost a love one, please stand by them.

Don't visit them one time and one time only. It is a long way to recover, and they can't do it alone.

Now, I want to take this time to thank all t hose who

read this book. I hope it has been very helpful. Pray that no one has to go through anything like this, but if you do or if you, have, this book will help you through it. But most of all, I want you to "Lean on God." Once again. I thank you!

THE END

This book has been dedicated in loving memory of Thomas Bernard Green, Jr. (Tommy J.)

Printed in the United States
By Bookmasters